From Roots to Bloom

Plants Have a Purpose

By Margaret Williamson

Discover Plants and Animals
Vowel Teams
(oo, ue)

Scan this code to access the Teacher's Notes for this series or visit
www.norwoodhousepress.com/decodables

NORWOOD HOUSE PRESS

DEAR CAREGIVER, *The Decodables* series contains books following a systematic, cumulative phonics scope and sequence aligned with the science of reading. Each book allows its reader to apply their phonics knowledge in engaging and relatable texts. The words within each text have been carefully selected to ensure that readers can rely on their decoding skills as they encounter new or unfamiliar words. They also include high frequency words appropriate for the target skill level of the reader.

When reading these books with your child, encourage them to sound out words that are unfamiliar by attending to the target letter(s) and sounds. If the unknown word is an irregularly spelled high frequency word or a word containing a pattern that has yet to be taught (challenge words) you may encourage your child to attend to the known parts of the word and provide the pronunciation of the unknown part(s). Rereading the texts multiple times will allow your child the opportunity to build their reading fluency, a skill necessary for proficient comprehension.

You can be confident you are providing your child with opportunities to build their decoding abilities which will encourage their independence as they become lifelong readers.

Happy Reading!

Emily Nudds, M.S. Ed Literacy
Literacy Consultant

Norwood House Press • www.norwoodhousepress.com
The Decodables ©2024 by Norwood House Press. All Rights Reserved.
Printed in the United States of America.
367N–082023

Library of Congress Cataloging-in-Publication Data has been filed and is available at https://lccn.loc.gov/2023010396

Literacy Consultant: Emily Nudds, M.S.Ed Literacy
Editorial and Production Development and Management: Focus Strategic Communications Inc.
Editors: Christine Gaba, Christi Davis-Martell
Photo Credits: Shutterstock: Addkm (p.5), Alexander_Safonov (p.11), Andreea Grosu (p.6), Barisev Roman (p.16), B Brown (p. 15), Hong Vo (p. 6), HVPMdev (p.6), hxdbzxy (p. 21), I.Luna (p.8), Irina Fischer (p. 5), JeniFoto (p. 7), Jerry Horbert (p. 18), Johnathan M. Thomas (p. 9), Juan Llauro (p. 17), Lana Langlois (p. 15), Ledy X (p. 21), Leo_nik (p. 19), Macrovector (covers), Madeleine Steinbach (cover, p. 9), Manusphoto (p. 19), Marc Bruxelle (p. 17), Maria Evseyeva (p. 6), Maria T Hoffman (p. 4), MothLady (p. 13), Nataly Studio (p. 9), Pearl PhotoPix (p. 20), Shablovskiystock (p. 15), Studio KIWI (p. 13), Subbotina Anna (p. 12), Tatiana Volgutova (p. 8), Tom Tietz (p. 14), vermontalm (p. 16), Yuriy Ivanovskiy (p. 10).

Hardcover ISBN: 978-1-68450-687-3   Paperback ISBN: 978-1-68404-903-5
eBook ISBN: 978-1-68404-958-5

Contents

Introduction:
The Scoop on Plants

From roots to bloom, people and animals need plants. Plants provide food. They offer shelter. They give the air a boost. They help keep the air clean. Plants even fuel other plants. It is true that plants are incredible.

Flowers bloom in a garden.

Lettuce, kale, and spinach leaves can be put in salads. Kale smoothies are very healthy.

This kale smoothie is ready to drink.

Blueberry pie is a yummy treat.

Fruits grow from the seeds and blooms of a plant.

Blueberries and gooseberries are fruits. They grow on bushes. They make ooey-gooey jams and pies.

You can put gooseberry jam on toast.

8

When we are in a blue mood we can feel sad.

Even some flower blooms are food. They can be brewed into soothing teas that can help a blue mood. Some boost the body's energy. Some can help the body snooze.

Many people drink chamomile tea.

Edible flowers bring color to a yummy salad.

Coconut oil can be used many ways.

The seeds of some plants are oily. They can be used to make cooking oil. Coconut oil is an oil that can be used in grooming, too. It makes hair shiny and smooth.

Peppers, tomatoes, and cucumbers are the fruits of their plants. Different types of squash are all fruits from plants, too.

Don't be fooled. A cucumber is a fruit. The clue? It grows from a flower.

This flower will grow a cucumber.

11

Plants As Healers

Plants can be used for healing. The gel in aloe vera leaves can be used to treat burns. Coneflowers are chopped, dried, and cooked to make medicine. Coneflower can be used to ease tooth pain or a sore throat.

Aloe vera leaves contain a gel that help burns to heal.

A dandelion is not all doom and gloom. It might be a weed, but it's a cool one. Every part of the dandelion is food. The cooked root can boost tummy health. The root can also be used to replace coffee. The leaves can wrap and soothe a cut.

Bees love dandelions.

Some people drink dandelion tea.

Trees Are a Type of Plant

Trees are the largest plants. Their branches droop over the forest. They put a roof over the heads of many animals.

The branches in a forest make a good home for a moose.

Lumber is a booming **industry**. Wood is used in every room of a house. Even a school desk can be made of wood. Paper is made from wood pulp. Toilet tissue looped in spools is made from wood pulp, too.

Planks of wood are part of the lumber industry.

This room in a log home is made of wood.

Paper products like tissue and sheets of paper are made from wood pulp.

Maple trees ooze sap in the spring, right at the end of winter. It is collected from trees in a sugar bush. Then it is made into sweet, smooth maple syrup.

The sap drips into buckets.

Sometimes sap drips into hoses.

Many people like to put a spoonful of maple syrup on their pancakes or waffles.

Maple sap can also be made into maple sugar and maple sugar candy. Too much candy can cause a toothache, though!

Blueberry pancakes with maple syrup is a yummy meal.

Hot syrup on snow makes a toffee treat.

Plants Are Always in Fashion

Clothing can be made from plants. Cotton is a plant. Its loose fluffy **boll** is used to make cloth. Cotton is a cool and soothing cloth. People snooze on sheets and pillowcases made with cotton.

Cotton bolls are used to make cotton.

Rubber can be made from tree sap. The sticky sap oozes from the tree.

Rubber from trees is used in many ways. It is in tires, rubber boots, and even balloons!

Rubber boots help keep out the wet.

Rubber sap can come from a rubber tree.

Green Spaces

Green spaces are important to the planet. Large green spaces in cities help to keep them cool. They reduce **noise pollution**. Plants and tree roots hold soil in place, too. This stops **erosion**.

Troops of hikers like green spaces for exercise.

People like green spaces.

Plants boost air quality. They need sunlight, water, and **carbon dioxide (CO$_2$)** to make their food. This process is called **photosynthesis**. Plants breathe in carbon dioxide from the air. They swoosh it away and store it. At night, once the food is made, the plant breathes out **oxygen (O$_2$)**. Animals and people need oxygen to live.

Even when a plant droops and dies, it continues to work. It becomes food for seeds and new plant shoots. It fuels the soil by adding moisture. It invites worms to turn the soil, keeping the flowers in bloom.

Plants are valued by people, animals, and other plants. Plants keep the soil healthy, make oxygen, and make food. We can use plants to make things we need, like tools, and they look beautiful, too. Plants have many purposes.

A young plant gets food from a stump.

Plants can be both useful and beautiful.

Glossary

boll (bōl): the part of a cotton plant that contains the seed

carbon dioxide (CO$_2$) (**kar**-bĭn dī-ŏk-sīd): an invisible gas that is in the air; used by plants during photosynthesis

erosion (ĭ-**rō**-zhən): occurs when soil is washed or blown away

green spaces: land that is covered with trees, plants, and grass

industry (**ĭn**-dŭ -strē): a group of companies that process raw materials and make them into products

lumber: wood or timber that has been cut into planks

noise pollution (noys-pŭ-**loo**-shŭn): unwanted or disturbing sound

oxygen (O$_2$) (**ŏk**-sĭ-jən): an invisible gas that is in the air; people must breathe it in to live

photosynthesis (fō-tō-**sĭn**-thə-sĭs): the process in which green plants use sunlight to make food

Index

Vowel Teams

oo

balloons	droops	mood	scoop	spools
bloom	food	proof	shoots	spoonful
booming	fooled	ooey-gooey	smooth	swoosh
boost	gloom	ooze	smoothies	too
boots	gooseberry	roof	snooze	tools
cool	looped	room	soothe	toothache
doom	loose	roots	soothing	troops

ue

blueberries	blue	tissue	true	valued

High-Frequency Words

air	give	live	over	very
animals	house	many	turn	work
even	large	new		

Challenging Words

burns	healthy	oil	rhubarb	tissue
chamomile	important	potatoes	squash	toilet
clothing	incredible	provide	stalks	toothache
energy	lettuce	replace	syrup	wood
exercise	moisture			

Lots of yummy treats grow in a vegetable garden.

People can enjoy plants in parks and gardens.

Plants As Food

We eat the roots of plants. Potatoes are proof.
We munch on plant stems and shoots, too.

Carrots are a yummy root.

Yucca roots are eaten by many people.

We can eat cooked rhubarb stalks for a treat.

Yams can also be called sweet potatoes.